Written and Dedicated to:

God,
My Mom,
and all those struggling from mental illness.

DARK SPACES

SHINING LIGHT ON MENTAL ILLNESS

CAMERON ROSE

iUniverse

DARK SPACES
SHINING LIGHT ON MENTAL ILLNESS

iUniverse books may be ordered through booksellers or by contacting:

iUniverse
1663 Liberty Drive
Bloomington, IN 47403
www.iuniverse.com
1-800-Authors (1-800-288-4677)

Because of the dynamic nature of the Internet, any web addresses or links contained in this book may have changed since publication and may no longer be valid. The views expressed in this work are solely those of the author and do not necessarily reflect the views of the publisher, and the publisher hereby disclaims any responsibility for them.

Any people depicted in stock imagery provided by Getty Images are models, and such images are being used for illustrative purposes only.
Certain stock imagery © Getty Images.

ISBN: 978-1-5320-9218-3 (sc)
ISBN: 978-1-5320-9219-0 (e)

Print information available on the last page.

iUniverse rev. date: 01/16/2020

CONTENTS

LOST IN THE DARKNESS

Lost in the Darkness will explore the emotions that people with mental illness feel daily with the hope that if you or someone you know are suffering from mental illness that these poems will help end the silence.

PART 1: THE VOID

When becoming Lost in the Darkness, it first starts with a feeling of emptiness. The feeling is often engulfing and suffocating for those that are caught in its grips. It brings even the mightiest to their knees, making you feel lost and alone. You feel trapped inside yourself, banging from inside your body to be set free, like a genie in a lamp. Except your only wish is for this emptiness to dissipate.

To those trapped in a never-ending darkness...

THE ABYSS

Imagine driving through a dark tunnel,
Now imagine driving through this dark tunnel
but it never seems to come to an end.
There is no light at the end,
Just continuous darkness.
It feels like a bad dream
that you're trying to wake up from.
But no matter how hard you try
you can never get out.
Then out of nowhere there's light,
You rejoice because you've come
out of the tunnel and into the light.
But you're still on guard, knowing
that at any moment,
You could be pushed back into the darkness.

LOST AND FOUND

Tucked away in the corner of the room,
I once was worn,
I once was used.
Surrounded by brown
and continuously pushed down,
I look to escape this makeshift home
that packages things unknown.

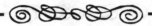

BLACK HOLE

The darkness approaches,
Peeling away, removing the light
that keeps me alive.
I try to fight but it's too overwhelming,
Consuming me from the inside out,
Concealing the me that wants to stay out.

Adrift…

LOST AT SEA

Floating above the waves
no shore within sight.
Taking a beating, becoming a slave
to the fear that's inside.
Trying to hold myself up
but my body grows weary.
Pushing harder and harder but I'm stuck,
Wondering if I'll make it with the future so bleary.
I cry out for help
hoping it isn't too late.
That I haven't hurt myself
by letting my pride get in the way of my escape.

PART 2: FEAR

The feeling of emptiness is only the beginning. It knows you are vulnerable and it speaks fear into you, letting you know how much you have failed and where you continually fail. It tells you that nobody cares about you and that getting help is a waste of time. It speaks to your fear of looking weak and isolates you further and further until you believe you are on an island of solitude all by yourself.

I'm afraid of looking weak…

THERAPY

talk about my problems,
why would I need to do that?
i am not sitting down
and spilling my guts.
what are they going to say that i don't already know?
i am depressed, well who isn't these days.
sure, i drink a little, but how is some quack
going to help me with that.
i don't need to talk to someone about my mood,
especially not with some old dude.
i can get through this on my own,
don't worry about me.

FAILURE

I look around and what do I see?
The perfect families all around me.
Nothing close to the family I've raised,
They skimmed from the top while I merely grazed.
The struggles are as vast and deep as the sea,
I fight against the tide but it's taking me further into the deep.
To be a good parent is what I want,
But the truth is there will be times when I'm not.
There will be times when my mental illness will win,
Turn me away from the parent I should've been.
I don't want to fail my kids,
But the tires have flooded, and I've started to skid.

I fear myself…

FEAR OF THE UNKNOWN

They ask me what I fear?
They ask me what keeps me awake at night?
It's not my highs
or my lows.
It's not snakes, spiders,
or even ghosts.
What I fear most is myself,
That I didn't do more than I should've.
I fear that my mental illness pushed everyone away
and that I'm the reason that our family shattered today.

PART 3: ESCAPE

When it's isolated you and trapped you in the darkness, it goes in for the kill. It puts you in a place where you search for an escape, something that will take the pain away. We think of freedom as gaining or regaining rights, but do we ever consider freedom as an escape from what we may deem an unbearable force. People look for a way to escape from the pain they deem unbearable because they see no other option.

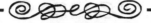

IF FREEDOM WAS…

If Freedom was a gun
I'd pull the trigger quick,
If Freedom was a pill
I'd make myself sick,
If Freedom was a noose
I'd tie it around my neck,
If Freedom was a drink
I'd throw it down the hatch,
If Freedom was a drug
I'd make another batch,
If Freedom was a car
I'd drive until I crash,
If Freedom was your voice
I'd make another choice,
If Freedom was your touch
I'd get out of bed,
If Freedom was your love
I might not be dead.

Setting sail for a new horizon...

THE HANGMAN'S NOOSE

Could today be the day
I take the leap of faith,
Cast my fears aside
I have nowhere else to hide.
The end draws near
as I shed my final tears,
It prickles my skin,
Tightening further around my throat.
Growing closer to the end
as I bring out the sails of the boat,
The brown surrounds
and the ship goes down.

Trying to numb the pain...

ALTERNATIVE MEDICINE

I look for a way to numb the pain,
I thought if I ignored it
it might dissipate.
No matter how hard I try
the pain always suffocates.
Restricting my lungs
and clogging my airways.
I search for a medicine that will help subdue
the pain and put it somewhere new.
The alcohol temporarily takes the pain away
but the feeling never stays.
Making me crave more and more
every single day.
I've lost myself to this endless bottle
but it only keeps my feelings at bay.
Searching for something else
that will take me to a new place...

EXPOSING THE DARKNESS

Mental illness is often seen as a taboo subject, one that is supposed to be kept silent because of how society views mental illness. Meanwhile, many suffer in silence and alone. Then when someone with mental illness kills themselves, we wonder why they never got help. *Lost in the Darkness* looked at the emotional side of mental illness. *Exposing the Darkness* will look at how people with mental illness are viewed by society and shed light on their struggles. It's time for people with mental illness to stop seeing themselves as burdens to society, but rather as the high functioning individuals they are.

PART 4: A SOCIETAL VIEW

Society has a great impact on how people with mental illness are seen. Often a negative light is cast upon those that struggle with mental illness. Misunderstanding accounts for a rather large portion because people don't always know the complexities that can come with mental illness. Poems in this section will shine a light on these misinterpretations and how society should view people with mental illness.

I don't fit into one category…

WHO HAS A MENTAL ILLNESS?

It's your neighbor,
It's your mom,
It's your dad,
It's your brother,
It's your sister,
It's your friend,
It's an actor,
It's a chef,
It's an athlete,
It's a CEO,
It's a grocery store clerk,
It's the mailman,
It's a secretary,
It has no specific race,
It has no specific face,
It has no specific gender,
It has no specific sexuality,
It affects everyone.

To my mom, you are strong…

UNWAVERING

You stand firm and tall
They try to bring you down
But you rise above them all,
Cast into the fire and left to die
Despite what's transpired
You found a way to survive,
Stronger and stronger you became
No spark was needed
To start that inner-flame,
The light at the end of my tunnel
You shine through the night
You became my funnel
Showed me what was wrong and right,
Doubt creeps in from all around,
You aren't good enough is
reverberated down!
But the right decision was made
Staying on earth and
Loving me each day,
Don't let others designate your worth
Stay strong and keep faith
You are where you belong
And there's no one else
I'm prouder to call my mom!

There is more than meets the eye…

THE SPECTRUM

They ask, *Are you sad?* Well then you must have depression,
Forgetting that sadness has more than one expression.
Misdiagnosis is bad, causing many to not get proper treatment,
Properly diagnosing is better than the possibility of bereavement.
The spectrum is broad between mania and depression,
With many not knowing that bipolar I and bipolar II are expressions.
There are highs and lows with bipolar I,
Manic Depression becoming more present in this one.
Bipolar II is much the same,
Highs and lows with Depression being the more insane.
The Spectrum is vast for every person around,
Never the same for those that are bound.

DEBBY DOWNER

What is wrong?
They say,
with much disdain.
You don't feel as if you belong?
These days seem so long?
You can't continue this way?
You're beginning to feel a bit insane?
This is your swan song?
Soon you'll be gone?

A lot is wrong,
I'm depressed, perhaps unsound.
At times I feel as if I don't belong,
it's hard to do a 180 and turn it all around.
This is my life until the day I die,
I won't be happy all of the time.
There will be good days and bad,
it's hard to be happy when I'm always sad.

The answer isn't always as easy as it seems...

I'M NOT LAZY

I know that the trash hasn't been taken out,
My mailbox is full and the mail keeps falling out.
The laundry has piled up and needs to be washed,
The dishes are dirty and so is the dishcloth.
I know I need to do it, but I can't get up,
My mind is telling my body that I've done enough.
When people see the mess that is my place,
A look of disgust falls over their face.
They wonder how I could let it get this bad,
It's hard to find motivation when you feel sad.
I wish they could put their feet in my shoes,
Then they might realize the struggles I go through.
I'm not lazy, I say,
But it falls on deaf ears, much to my dismay.
I'm not lazy...

PART 5: THE STRUGGLES

Those that suffer from mental illness are often misunderstood, as their struggles often affect their daily interactions with others. They want to feel safe being themselves around others but don't want to feel like a burden. We can see it as them distancing themselves from us, but often they are fighting against the complexities of their mental illness. Finding a way to forgive themselves and be comfortable with who they are can be the hardest part.

BIPOLAR

Today is a good day
but how long will it last,
I'm happy for a moment
and in the next it's passed.
The highs, the lows,
they come and they go,
Never quite knowing
which one will show?
A week at a time, sometimes two,
The mood I'm in affects what I do.
I'm already tired and it's only noon,
wishing this day will come to an end soon.
Take your meds and you'll be okay,
forget about the side effects,
you won't get tired or gain weight.
The Doctor prescribed it you'll be okay!
Treated as weak and fragile
by those who see mental illness as mindless babble.
Nobody chooses to be this way,
unable to control their emotions for the day.
My mood may change more often than yours
but it doesn't mean I'm incapable of doing more.
Treat me with respect and see me as your equal,
not as something lower than people.

THE WAVE

It comes crashing in out of nowhere
Making you subservient to its every command;
The weak shall parish and the mighty will stand.
That's what they say, but they don't know
how cunning and witty it is.
Elusive to the touch,
To escape is a privilege very few know,
Most sit in the dark
On a talk many refuse to start,
It whispers in your ear,
Tells you things you don't want to hear,
Inside it lingers
Invisible to the eye,
If you could see it, less would die.

Why aren't you here...?

ONE DAY AT A TIME

I keep asking myself,
Why am I this way?
I want to get out of bed
but everything in my body
tells me to stay put instead.
My friends are out having fun
but I'm in my room alone
and in the dark.
I don't want to go out
and my friends don't understand why.
They don't understand why I have been this way
for over a week.
Why would I choose to be by myself
instead of hanging out with them.
It's never easy to escape the void,
It's not something that you can just avoid.

It's easier keeping it locked inside...

WALKING ON EGGSHELLS

I'm walking around hoping no one sees
the darker side of me.
I want to be brave
but who can I trust to take this to the grave?
People will try to make me feel less
cause it's harder for me to handle stress.
Use the information they've received
as ammunition to turn my words into disbelief.
I want to be strong
but I feel lost in a world where I don't belong.
Hoping someday I won't have to worry
about the real me I had to bury.

Looking in all the wrong places…

SEARCHING FOR FORGIVENESS

I'm looking for comfort from all the wrong people,
Placing my faith in others instead of the steeple.
Who are those people whose opinions I care so much about?
The ones who ignore my screams and shouts.
I search for forgiveness for who I am,
Hoping that these people I don't know will be the solution to my plan.
Knowing that their love will never be enough,
But hoping it might help subdue the feelings of disgust.
I get down on my knees and pray,
Wondering if the Lord will take this curse away.
Why did I have to be the one?
What did I do to deserve this?
I search for forgiveness,
But it starts with forgiving myself.

BECOMING THE LIGHT IN DARK SPACES

Self-harm or attempting *suicide* is the most drastic measure that one can take with mental illness. Often those that seek this have reached a point in which they see no alternative. The truth is that they are wanting help but feel burdensome. We all know friends, family, or acquaintances that have attempted or completed suicide. Often signs were given for someone to help prevent these attempts, but someone missed them or was afraid to say something. *Becoming the Light in Dark Spaces* will discuss ways to help prevent someone from committing suicide and promote you to become a light that exposes the lies that tell them they shouldn't live any longer.

PART 6: BECOMING THE LIGHT

Suicide is seen as the last option for someone that is struggling with mental illness. There are ways to help people struggling to never see this as an option. It starts with exposing the lies that they've been told and told themselves. Being someone that provides wisdom and truth to someone in a dark place is quintessential to keep them from walking down a path toward suicide. The poems in this section will discuss ways to become a light in dark places.

OFFER A SOLUTION

Therapy,
Hearing this word brings two reactions,
Evoking disgust for some,
Rejoicement for those that know its powers.
Against all the hearsay and the nonbeliever's, therapy
Provides a safe place for those in need of release.
You don't know until you try, it could save a life.

BECOMING THE LIGHT

Be the light that shines through the dark,
Think of a fire in need of a spark.
Guide the blind toward the light,
Let them feel the warmth of the sun shining bright.
Away from the darkness, steer them clear,
No matter how much they listen to fear.
Trials and tribulations, you will face,
Be warm and helpful without invading their space.
Don't make them feel like they are a burden,
Turn yourself into a friendly curtain.
Keeping the darkness from peering in at night,
But letting them know you can bring light into their life.

THE GUIDING LIGHT

Place your faith in the one who saves,
the one who rose and conquered the grave.
The one who forgave your iniquities,
created you with such simplicity.
You are searching for a cure to take the pain away,
placing your faith in everything except his grace.
Believing you have been cursed,
forgetting that you have a purpose on this earth.
The lord doesn't make mistakes,
turn to him in your time of need and he can help relieve the ache.
It will not be easy, but nothing ever is,
if you seek to be fulfilled turn yourself over to him.
For he is the cure to your daily struggles,
take off the shrink wrap and pop all the bubbles.

A VOICE OF REASON

Speak words of wisdom,
Speak words of change,
The words you use
have more power than a mage.
The tongue is small
but its power is grand.
Can bring someone to their knees
and cause others to stand.
Be the shepherd
that guides the flock.
Taking them to pastures
and away from the rocks.

STAND BY ME

Be the one who stays,
They may try to push you away.
It might make it easier for them to be alone,
So they'll try to push out of their home.

Be the one who breaks down the walls,
The ones they've put up for so long.
To keep the hurt at bay,
Because they've never had anyone willing to stay.

Be the one who shows them they are strong,
That they are in a place where they belong.
That they are bigger than their fears and struggles,
With or without you they are capable of rebuttal.

Stand by them through thick and thin,
You don't know the things through which they have been.
Be the shoulder on which they can lean,
It could make a bigger difference than what you may think.

Melt away the ice…

SALT IN THE WOUND

Frozen to the core because
the storm made them cold.
Holding them under the water
and burying them in snow.
Keeping them trapped
inside their pain and
showing no sign of giving way.
The storm is all encompassing
but it can be broken through.
It starts with putting them before you,
and putting some salt on top of the wound.
Melting away the ice that's inside,
freeing them from the icy prison they built.
Be the salt they need,
so that one day they can be freed.

PART 7: PREVENTION

Suicide can become the only option someone suffering from mental illness sees available, but there are steps that you or they can take to prevent them from taking their life. The goal of these poems in this section will be to provide you with ways to potentially help save a person's life while offering a way for those who may be suffering to seek help.

Listen for more than what you hear…

HIDDEN AGENDA

It will start with, *I am okay.*

People don't need to be worried about me,
Last thing I want to do is burden someone with my problems,
All my problems are overwhelming,
Nobody needs more on their plate because of me.

Try and understand their problems,
Open your ears and listen.

Kill themselves they may,
If nobody is willing to intervene,
Listen to their fears and
Listen for the words untold.

Maybe
You are the
Someone that
Elicits
Love
For themselves that day.

SILENCE SPEAKS LOUDER THAN WORDS

Close your mouth,
Open your ears,
Open your eyes,
Listen to their fears,
Give a shoulder,
Give a hand,
Don't speak,
Try and understand,
Solutions and plans
Come as they may
Aren't always needed
For that day,
Listen for the words untold,
They won't always come printed in bold,
When it's time to ask, ask away,
You could save a life that day,
Close your mouth,
Open your eyes,
Open your ears,
Listen every time.

ASK THE QUESTION NO ONE ELSE WILL

Question their intentions,
You don't know
what someone may be thinking about doing.
Ask the question that you may not want to ask;
Are you thinking about killing yourself?
It may feel uncomfortable
but it could save a life.
If they say, *yes,*
Persuade them not to do it.
Clear out the lies
and noise pollution.
Fill their mind with love
and help them realize that this isn't the solution.
Refer them to someone that can help,
You can't do this by yourself.
They may accept, they may decline,
Don't force it on them, let them decide.
Stick around and help,
Your actions could save a life.

Know you are loved...

HOTLINE TO SAVE A LIFE

Know there are options for help
when you think you're by yourself.
There are things you can seek
that will help you reprieve.
People that will talk you down
and let you know you are wanted around.
Save your valuable life
by calling this number 1-800-273-8255
when the time is right.

CLOSING STATEMENTS

I hope *Dark Spaces* has brought more clarity to the world of mental illness. Mental illness affects people every day, and I hope that these poems have provided those who may not have a good understanding of mental illness more clarity and for those who are suffering from mental illness a pathway to get help if needed. You are more loved and valuable than you think!

Printed in the United States
By Bookmasters